Bromeli

A Wisley handbook

Bill Wall

Cassell
The Royal Horticultural Society

Cassell Educational Limited
Artillery House, Artillery Row
London SW1P 1RT
for the Royal Horticultural Society

First published 1988

British Library Cataloguing in Publication Data

Wall, Bill, 1924–
  Bromeliads.
  1. Indoor plants: Bromeliads
  I. Title   II. Royal Horticultural Society
  III. Series
  635.9′3422

  ISBN 0–304–32197–4

Photographs by Bill Wall and Michael Warren
Line drawings by Graham Wall
Design by Lesley Stewart

Phototypesetting by Chapterhouse Ltd, Formby
Printed in Hong Kong by Wing King Tong Co. Ltd

Contents

The silvery leaves of *Tillandsia argentea* are typical of the many so-called air plants

Introduction

The bromeliad family comprises over 2,000 species in more than 20 genera, all originating from South and Central America and the southern states of the USA, except for a solitary species of *Pitcairnia*, *P. feliciana*, discovered in West Africa in 1937. They have a common growth habit, the few or many leaves forming a rosette, which may be upright or flat, and in some cases making a cup in the centre that holds water, as in the familiar *Aechmea fasciata* or urn plant. Given such a large number of species, it is not surprising that bromeliads are found in widely different situations: they are distributed in nature at altitudes ranging from sea level in the tropics to the heights of the South American Andes, living in conditions of high humidity on the forest floor or in arid desert and growing on trees or in the ground. As a result, they vary enormously in appearance, from the tiny mat-forming rosettes of *Abromeitiella* to the giant *Brocchinia* and *Puya*. Within the genus *Tillandsia* alone there is great variation, from hard stiff-leaved plants growing on cacti, to the lichen-like Spanish moss, *T. usneoides*, which hangs from trees and is so characteristic of the moist southern states of the USA.

The flower heads of bromeliads are also very diverse, with the small white flowers of *Cryptanthus* almost hidden in the leaf axils, the flamboyant red and yellow flower spikes of *Guzmania*, the blue and green of *Puya* and the yellow flowers that protrude from waxy-looking bract spikes of *Vriesea*. All, though, are characterized botanically by having three-petalled flowers and three-celled ovaries. The flower spike, with very few exceptions, appears from the centre of the rosette and, after flowering, the rosette ceases to grow but produces new plants from dormant buds in the leaf axils. The leaves of the majority of species have tiny shield-like scales, which are able to absorb moisture from the air and help the plant survive drought or extreme heat. Some bromeliads have only two scales at the base of each leaf, while others have numerous scales forming grey bands across the leaves. In many *Tillandsia*, the leaf surface is almost entirely covered with scales, giving the whole plant a silver scurfy appearance.

The first bromeliad introduced to Britain was the pineapple, *Ananas comosus*, in 1690. In Victorian times it was grown to perfection in hothouses and specially constructed hotbeds of manure, to grace the tables of the wealthy. Further introductions followed slowly and large collections had been established in Europe by the

× *Neomea* 'Popcorn', an example of an inter-generic hybrid between *Neoregelia* and *Aechmea*

end of the nineteenth century. Sadly, during the two world wars, these were gradually dispersed and lost, although some of the hybrids produced then do still exist and stocks have also been renewed from those that survived.

Since the 1940s, hundreds of new species have been introduced into cultivation, both in Europe and the USA. As bromeliads are readily hybridized and grown from seed, numerous hybrids have been raised too, not only within a particular genus but between different genera, such as *Aechmea* × *Neoregelia* and *Cryptanthus* × *Billbergia*. Bromeliads have become increasingly popular and are now common as houseplants and for decorating foyers, offices and shopping complexes. They are tough plants, able to withstand a considerable amount of neglect and remain colourful under quite harsh conditions. The number of plants available commercially has also increased by leaps and bounds and, whereas in 1950 it would have been quite difficult to obtain examples of more than a dozen species, today it would not be much of a problem to collect 100 different species and hybrids.

General cultivation

Temperature

Bromeliads may be grown to perfection in a greenhouse or conservatory. The range of plants that can be accommodated depends on the winter minimum temperature. If this is maintained at 60°F (15°C), then all the species and hybrids will succeed. A lower temperature of 50°F (10°C) will limit the number to some extent and 40°F (5°C) even more, although there is still a wide choice of plants. The temperature requirements of individual plants are given in their descriptions in each chapter. As a rough guide, the softer-leaved kinds need a higher temperature, while those with very hard, stiff leaves are much more tolerant of cold. The soft-leaved types include *Guzmania*, most *Vriesea* and some of the *Aechmea* and *Tillandsia*. *Cryptanthus* are also warmth-loving, originating as they do from the forest floor. In a cool greenhouse, most *Aechmea*, *Billbergia*, *Neoregelia*, *Dyckia* and *Puya* can be grown and many of the grey-leaved xerophytic (existing with little water) *Tillandsia*. The intermediate temperature allows numerous *Aechmea*, *Nidularium* and *Pitcairnia* to be added to those listed for the cool greenhouse.

Light

Under glass, we can provide the right environment for any bromeliad by careful positioning. Some light shading, as produced by a coat of Summercloud on the outside of the glass, is advisable to prevent direct sunshine scorching the plants. Place the light-loving xerophytic *Tillandsia* and *Dyckia* and the hard-leaved *Aechmea* and *Billbergia* high up, where they get most light, followed in decreasing order of light intensity by *Neoregelia*, *Pitcairnia*, *Guzmania*, soft-leaved *Aechmea* and *Tillandsia*, *Nidularium* and *Cryptanthus*. All bromeliads will grow in shade or semi-shade, but the stiff-leaved types have a much better shape and leaf colour when given plenty of light; on the other hand, many of the coloured-leaved *Vriesea* and *Guzmania* bleach and lose their exotic appearance in too much light. Light, therefore, is one of the most important factors in bromeliad culture.

9

Nidularium species, such as N. fulgens, require temperatures above 50°F (10°)

Composts, potting and watering

Moisture is also important. The xerophytic Tillandsia or air plants are characterized by grey-scaled leaves and are epiphytic (tree-dwelling) in nature, most of them relying on heavy dews at night for water. Under glass, it is necessary to ensure extremely rapid drainage of excess water and good air circulation, thus enabling them to dry out and allowing the peltate (shield-like) scales on the leaves to retain sufficient water for the plants to use for a day or so. They are best grown mounted on a piece of bark or branch hung up in the greenhouse (see p.12).

Other bromeliads, like Dyckia and Hechtia, are succulent terrestrial (growing on the ground) plants and can store water in their fleshy leaves for some time. They should be potted into a very open compost of equal volumes of coarse sand and moss peat and watered only when completely dry.

The remaining bromeliads – the majority – can be grown in pots using a mixture of coarse sand and moss peat in equal volumes, plus half a part of leafmould. This affords the free drainage they all need. The compost should always be allowed to dry out between waterings and feeding with a high potash liquid fertilizer, such as Tomorite, at every third watering will bring out the

Opposite: the soft-leaved Vriesea nana does best in good light

best colour in the leaves, without producing a lot of soft leaf growth. Plastic or clay pots may be used. Clay is particularly suitable for bromeliads, since it permits air to reach the roots – an important factor with epiphytic plants, which most bromeliads are. In addition, clay is heavier than plastic and makes the plants much more stable in their pots.

In the greenhouse or conservatory, particularly with a large permanent collection, the easiest method of watering is a hose-pipe fitted with a spray nozzle. The central cup or vase of bromeliads can be flushed out with plenty of water, to prevent possible stagnation when the flower spike has finished flowering and is beginning to rot away. The question is often asked whether the cup of a bromeliad should be kept full of water. There is in fact no need to do so, but water must be supplied to the roots as with all other plants. Water that does get into the cup will not hurt the plant and under normal conditions helps to maintain some humidity. However, if the temperature is likely to fall below 40°F (5°C) at any time, the liquid should be tipped out, otherwise a "cold burn" may form on the foliage at the level of the water, which will show as a brown line across each leaf when the plant as grown on.

Permanent planting

An excellent way to grow bromeliads in the greenhouse or conservatory is in a permanent bed specially designed for them. This is easily constructed with wooden boards about 9 in. (23 cm) wide, which are placed on the floor of the greenhouse to make a rectangular frame of the required size. Set a couple of dead tree branches or artificial trees (see below) in the middle and then put a layer of broken brick in the bottom of the frame to a depth of about 3 in. (7.5 cm). Finally, fill the frame with a mixture of equal volumes of coarse sand and moss peat. The trees may be planted with *Tillandsia* and other epiphytic plants and the bed below can house the more shade-loving bromeliads. Many other plants, like begonias, gesnerias and ferns, will also thrive in such a planting.

Making a bromeliad tree

As suggested earlier, a small "tree" is very good for displaying bromeliads in the greenhouse or conservatory or even in the home. It can be simply made with cork bark, which is available from florists and garden centres.

For a small artificial tree 2½ ft (75 cm) or so high, make up a framework of crumpled chicken wire to the rough shape of tree

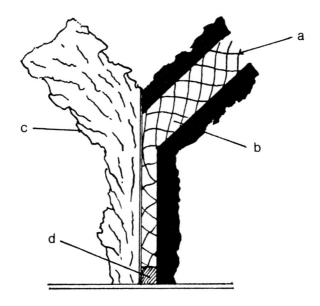

Figure 1: construction of a bromeliad tree
(a)   Crumpled wire mesh framework
(b)   Interior filled with foam plastic
(c)   Cork bark
(d)   Cement base

desired (see figure 1). Place the bottom of the framework in a mixture consisting of two parts of sand to one of cement, in a 5 in. (12.5 cm) half-pot, and leave it to dry for a day or two. The plastic half-pot can then be removed, having served its function as a mould. This gives a "tailor's dummy" on to which sections of cork bark can be wired or glued, using a silicone sealant or adhesive. Make sure the lower pieces of bark are well attached to the cement base. Next, cover any gaps or holes between the pieces of bark by pinning on strips of polythene sheet. The tree may then be filled with a polymeric foam filler, which is sold by DIY shops for thermal insulation. To use it, two chemicals are mixed together and the resultant foaming liquid is poured into the inside of the tree, where it quickly expands and hardens to fill all the spaces and give a rigid structure. After an hour, unpin the pieces of polythene and trim off any excess hardened foam with a knife. Visible foam surfaces can be painted brown to blend with the cork bark. An alternative method is to pack the bark tree with chunks of plastic foam, of the type used for cushions.

Provision should be made for medium-sized bromeliads by

nailing on some curved pieces of bark to form pockets, which will contain the roots. *Aechmea, Billbergia, Neoregelia* and *Nidularium* can be planted in these pockets, using a mixture of sphagnum moss and moss peat and covering the surface with a layer of sphagnum moss alone. Epiphytic and xerophytic plants are prepared by covering their roots with a ball of sphagnum moss and tying or nailing these to the bark tree. Some of the very grey-leaved *Tillandsia* may be attached simply by glueing the base on to the bark with a silicone adhesive.

Once it is assembled and planted, water the whole tree thoroughly, using a can fitted with a fine rose, and allow it to drain. If intended for the home, the tree is best stood in a saucer or dish to avoid marking the shelf or table underneath it. Further watering should be carried out at intervals, according to the appearance of the sphagnum moss. When the moss is green and obviously damp, water is not needed, but when it becomes whitish in colour and crisp to the touch, water should be given. Rainwater is preferable, using a fine spray and making sure that the whole assembly is soaked. The addition of a high potash liquid fertilizer at every third watering is recommended.

Planted with bromeliads that remain fairly compact, the tree will last for several years and may be moved about between greenhouse and home without difficulty. Good plants for the purpose are the smaller *Billbergia, Crypthanthus, Vriesea carinata, Guzmania lingulata,* × *Cryptbergia rubra,* the dwarf *Neoregelia* and, if the tree can be kept in a very light position, the grey-leaved *Tillandsia.* In a greenhouse, larger plants of many genera may also be accommodated.

IN THE HOME

Bromeliads are ideal houseplants. They are colourful and long-lasting in flower, often with coloured foliage as well. The leaves are resilient and not easily damaged and the plants are tolerant of a wide range of temperature, humidity and light conditions, even putting up with erratic watering, to which houseplants are often subjected. They are generally bought in flower, sometimes with instructions from the florist to water only the central cup and not the compost in the pot. They should, however, be treated just like other plants, watering the compost when necessary – that is, when it has become dry. There is no need to keep the centre of a plant like *Aechmea fasciata* full of water, particularly if there is any risk of it being accidentally knocked over on to the carpet!

Many bromeliads are purchased on sight and then thrown away when the flower spike becomes brown, usually after weeks

The well-known *Guzmania lingulata*, an easy houseplant and also
suitable for a bromeliad tree

or even months of display. However, a plant can easily be kept, in order to grow offsets and produce new plants (see p.18). Alternatively, it may be grown into a bigger multi-headed plant. To do this, remove the old flower and repot the plant in a pot 2 in. (5 cm) larger than the previous one. As the flower spike begins to die off, offsets will be produced from the leaf axils. Continue watering as normal and give a high potash fertilizer at every third watering. The old flower spike should be removed once it is dead and, whenever any of the old leaves begin to die back, these too may be detached, although many of them will persist and remain in good condition for some months. After about a year in the case of *Aechmea fasciata*, the plant will have formed a two- or three-headed specimen which, if kept in a fairly light position, may well produce a flower spike from each of the rosettes in their second year. Other commonly offered species and hybrids of *Aechmea*, *Guzmania*, *Neoregelia*, *Nidularium* and *Vriesea* may be treated in the same way, apart from *Vriesea splendens*, the flaming sword, which is usually grown from seed to flower and then discarded.

Almost without exception, bromeliads are very easy houseplants. The various species and hybrids of *Billbergia* are probably the toughest of all and will stand the lowest temperatures, while *Vriesea*, *Guzmania* and *Cryptanthus* revel in warm conditions. In recent years, a large number of xerophytic *Tillandsia* have become available, mounted on various bases like seashells and pieces of driftwood (although I am rather apprehensive about the use of shells because of their alkaline reaction). These air plants should thrive and flower if they are kept in a light position indoors and dipped or sprayed with rainwater daily, adding liquid fertilizer to the water at every third watering during the summer.

Further information about cultivation, together with brief descriptions of some readily available plants, is given in the chapters devoted to specific groups and genera.

Opposite, above: *Neoregelia meyendorffii* var. *tricolor* may be kept and grown on into a larger plant

Below: the dwarf *Tillandsia ionantha* var. *scaposa* is usually grown on a piece of bark

17

Propagation

Bromeliads are propagated by means of offsets or from seed.

OFFSETS

The easiest, almost foolproof way to increase bromeliads is by offsets or "pups", produced from a plant usually just before and for
some time after flowering. This is, of course, the only method of
propagating particular forms, such as variegated ones, and
named hybrids.

With most bromeliads, the flower spike arises from the centre
of the tube or rosette that makes up the plant and, having
flowered, the rosette will not flower again. After flowering time,
the plant begins to grow suckers from one or more of its lower leaf
axils. Some species produce their pups close to the axils, while
others have a long woody stem or stolon bearing a new rosette at
its tip (see figures 2 and 3). Whatever the habit, when a pup has
reached about a third of the size of its parent rosette, it may be
detached quite easily with a sideways pressure of the thumb. It
should then be potted into a mixture of equal volumes of coarse
sand and moss peat in a small pot, watered in and grown on in the
normal conditions suitable for the plant concerned. Subsequent
watering is carried out at intervals and only when the compost is
dry. Be careful not to allow water into the centre of the new
rosette before it is rooted, or it might become "blind" and will not
grow on. Even so, a blind pup will in time produce its own small
offset, which will become your new plant, although later than if it
had been the original pup.

Offsets may also be rooted while they are still attached to the
parent plant. When the pup has attained about one quarter of the
size of the parent, the stolon is covered with a peat and sand
mixture for a month or so. Roots form very freely from the bottom
of the pup and it is taken off and potted up once it is obviously
growing in its own right.

A plant generally produces one to three pups initially and, even
after these have been removed, the parent can be retained. Its
leaves may become rather tatty, but they can be trimmed back so
that the plant takes up a minimum of space. This old stump will
last anything up to three or four years, during which time it will
produce further pups at intervals, with the possibility of giving

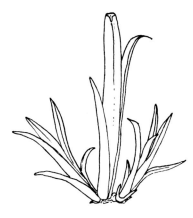

Figure 2: a typical billbergia with offsets produced from near the base of the parent plant

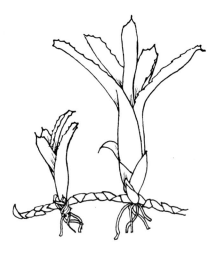

Figure 3: a bromeliad which makes new rosettes at the end of long stolons is characteristic of the creeping types of *Neoregelia*

one pup from a bud at the base of every leaf. The offsets will root in a peat and sand mixture at any time of year, provided the temperature is suitable for the particular plant being propagated.

The time taken for the new plants to come into flower varies with the species. Most *Billbergia* and a few *Aechmea* will flower one year after detaching the offset, remembering that each type has its own season of flowering. Others take two years, including many of the smaller *Aechmea*, *Neoregelia*, *Nidularium*, *Guzmania* and *Vriesea*, and *Tillandsia* take anything from one to ten years.

19

Vriesea splendens and one or two closely related species are rather different in their behaviour. After flowering, they form only one offset, from a bud near the centre of the old rosette, which is difficult to remove and root separately. As it grows, the old leaves tend to die off fairly quickly and the new growth is left on the old stump to grow on and flower. For this reason, plants are usually raised from seed.

Cryptanthus species and hybrids produce their offsets liberally from the leaf axils, in some cases without the parent plant coming into flower. The tiny pups are very easily detached – in fact they almost fall off by themselves – and, if potted into a peat and sand mixture, will grow and even produce pups themselves without developing any roots. *Cryptanthus* generally like warm moist conditions and seem to need a bottom heat of about 65°F (18°C) to form a good root system.

The silver-leaved xerophytic *Tillandsia* may also be increased by offsets, but not as simply as most other bromeliads. After flowering, they produce offsets from the leaf axils, usually very close to the base of a leaf and therefore more awkward to detach from the parent. It is best to leave the pup until it is about half the size of the adult plant, by which time it has probably got a couple of wiry roots. The lower leaves on the old plant should then be stripped off to reveal the pup, which can be carefully teased away and tied or stuck to a piece of wood or bark.

SEED

Bromeliad seeds are of three kinds. *Aechmea*, *Billbergia* and related genera form small berries after the flowers have been fertilized, which are full of a sticky jelly enclosing the seeds. This jelly must be washed off the seeds before they are dried and sown, preferably rinsing them first with a solution of half-strength fungicide to prevent any fungal growths. Other bromeliads, like *Pitcairnia* and the terrestrial *Puya* and *Dyckia*, produce seed capsules containing free dry seeds that are easily harvested. Finally, epiphytic plants such as *Tillandsia*, *Vriesea* and *Guzmania* have dry seeds with silken parachutes, rather like dandelion seed, which are dispersed by the wind in nature.

Non-winged bromeliad seeds of the first two types can be sown on the surface of a mixture of equal parts of fine moss peat and coarse sand, the compost half filling a small plastic tray, and should be lightly watered with a very fine rose, adding fungicide to the water. Place a sheet of glass over the tray, cover this with a sheet of paper and put it in a heated propagator at 70°–80°F (21°–26°C). Germination normally takes from one to three weeks, during which time the seed bed should be kept moist but not soggy, watering with a fungicide solution.

Once the seeds have germinated, the sheet of paper should be removed and, as the seedlings grow, the glass may be gradually opened from the tray, still keeping this in the propagator. When the seedlings reach a height of about 1 in. (2.5 cm), transplant them to a 3 in. (7.5 cm) pot, spacing them about ⅜ in. (1 cm) apart in a compost of moss peat and coarse sand in equal volumes. The pot should be returned to the propagator for a week or so, after which the seedlings can be hardened off to a temperature of about 60°F (15°C). Keep the pot in a lightly shaded position, water only when almost dry and feed with a half-strength liquid fertilizer at every third watering, until the seedlings are large enough to pot on into individual 3 in. (7.5 cm) pots of the same compost.

Winged seeds of the third type are treated differently. They are sown on the surface of a mixture of sand and chopped live sphagnum moss, or on a bundle of rough-barked twigs like conifer, and kept shaded and moist in a heated propagator at 70°–80°F (21°–26°C). It is essential to ensure moist conditions at all times and to use a fungicide such as cheshunt compound. The seedlings are slow-growing and will take several months to reach a sufficient size for transplanting. When large enough, they should be taken from their germination site and either put on to small pieces of twig or fern root, for xerophytic plants, or planted in a moss peat and sand mixture, for stronger plants like *Vriesea splendens* and *Tillandsia lindenii*. Keep these seedlings in the propagator for several weeks until they have rooted and established themselves. Then grow them on in light shade at 65°F (18°C), feeding with half-strength liquid fertilizer at every third watering.

Pests and diseases

Bromeliads are remarkably free from diseases. As very young seedlings, they may be overcome occasionally by mould, but the use of a suitable fungicide (see p.21) at this early stage is an effective control. Once plants are about three months old, the danger of fungal attack seems to be past, as long as they are grown at the appropriate temperature for the particular plants. Tropical plants like *Vriesea* and *Guzmania* can rot at the crown if subjected to very low temperatures, say 40°F (5°C), particularly if water is retained in the centre. However, temperatures as high as 100°F (37°C) do not seem to trouble bromeliads at all.

Of the pests, scale insects will attack bromeliads, appearing as small round or oval limpet-like objects on the leaves. The young insects are able to move about freely and spread across the leaves and to other plants, before settling down to produce a batch of young. They multiply rapidly and not only make a plant very unsightly, by producing yellow spots on the leaves where they suck the sap, but greatly weaken it if allowed to accumulate, which they can do at the base of the clasping leaves of a bromeliad. Treatment consists of spraying with malathion or, better still, with one of the modern systemic insecticides, and it is possible to eliminate them quite easily.

Mealybug and more particularly root mealybug, which are both characterized by their cotton-wool protective covering, may be dealt with in the same way.

Slugs and snails will eat young seedlings if given the chance. They often find a home in the damp, clasping, leaf bases of the rosettes of adult plants, emerging at night to feast on the flower spikes (not usually the leaves, which seem to be too tough) or on other plants. Watch out for them and use slug bait if necessary.

Aechmea

Aechmeas constitute a large genus of bromeliads and are widely distributed in nature from Mexico to Argentina. Nearly all of them form strong open rosettes, often retaining water in the centre of the plant. They have good root systems, which not only anchor them to their hosts – for they are mostly epiphytic – but take in sustenance from the rotting detritus that accumulates in pockets on the trees where they grow. The flower heads are very showy and remain so over a long period, although each individual floret lasts only a day or two. The flowers may be white, yellow, pink, red or purple and emerge from brilliantly coloured bracts, often of a different colour. Berried fruits are produced after flowering and these are usually highly coloured and last for several months.

Aechmeas are all very easy to grow and are excellent houseplants, able to accept the low humidity that generally prevails indoors. They are best given a light position in normal living room conditions, where they will grow throughout the year. This means that they need to be watered in winter and summer and fed with a high potash fertilizer at every third watering. Quite small pots may be used for bromeliads relative to the size of the plant, the main criterion being to ensure stability. For most of the smaller *Aechmea*, forming a rosette up to 1½ft (45 cm) diameter, a 5 in. (12.5 cm) clay pot or a 5½ in. (14 cm) plastic half-pot is sufficient and a compost of equal volumes of moss peat and coarse sand is suitable.

In the greenhouse, the same compost may be used for plants grown in pots and they should be positioned to receive as much light as possible, but without direct sunlight shining on them through the glass. A winter minimum temperature of 45°F (7°C) will do for the stiff-leaved kinds, if they are kept fairly dry, and applies in the descriptions below unless otherwise stated. However, those like *Aechmea fulgens* and *A.* 'Foster's Favorite', which have thinner, more flexible leaves, require 50°F (10°C) or more. All can be grown on a bromeliad tree.

After flowering, most *Aechmea* produce their offsets on strong woody stolons, often several inches long. This allows the development of new rosettes without congestion if a specimen multi-headed plant is wanted (see p.17), or the offsets may be detached and potted as separate plants (see p.18).

A. chantinii. This beautiful Amazonian species consists of an open rosette of about a dozen leaves, which are 2 in. (5 cm) broad and 1 ft (30 cm) long, decorated with broad bands of green and white. In August it bears a dense panicle of red and yellow flowers surrounded by bright red bracts. Sometimes available from florists, it is a good houseplant but should have a winter minimum temperature of 60°F (15°C).

A. cylindrata. This has a long cylindrical flower spike in June, up to 9 in. (23 cm) long and 2 in. (5 cm) in diameter, of rose-pink bracts enclosing pale blue flowers, which are followed by long-lasting pink berries. It is one of the smaller *Aechmea*, with a rosette 1½ ft (45 cm) in diameter, comprising firm green leaves edged with small brown spines. It comes from Brazil.

A. fasciata. Probably the best known member of the genus is the urn plant, which forms an open rosette 2 ft (60 cm) across of very stiff, grey-green, spine-edged leaves, banded with silver-grey. The leaves are 2 to 3 in. (5–7.5 cm) wide and form a central cup or vase which will retain water. The flower head rises from the centre of the rosette to make a stiff, rather solid-looking arrangement of light purple flowers surrounded by prickly pink bracts and bract leaves. This showy flower spike lasts for several months under a wide range of temperatures, from 45°F (7°C) to 100°F (37°C).

A. 'Foster's Favorite'. This is one of the most popular hybrids, with about 20 narrow, glossy, wine-red leaves 1 ft (30 cm) long, slightly recurving to form a small rosette. The drooping panicle of blue and orange flowers appears in summer, later giving way to coral-red berries. It should have a minimum winter temperature of 50°F (10°C). There is also a variegated form with stripes of white along the leaf blades, but, like most variegated bromeliads, it is not easy to obtain since plants must be propagated by offsets.

A. fulgens. This Brazilian species has a large spike of violet flowers contained in bright orange-red bracts. The florets turn red as they age and are succeeded by round, red, shining berries. It is one of the soft-leaved types, with 1 ft (30 cm) leaves, green on top and with a grey wax-like coating underneath. The variety *discolor* has dark wine-red leaves. A temperature of 50°F (10°C) is necessary in winter and rather less light than for most aechmeas.

A. gamosepala. A tough rosette of 1 ft (30 cm) leaves, greyish below and tinged at the base with black-purple, this is one of the easiest aechmeas to grow. The flower is an open spike of rose-pink and blue in June and July, followed by round pink berries, the whole held well above the leaves.

A. nudicaulis. This is one of the aechmeas that form tall upright tubes. The few leaves are 1 to 3 ft (30–90 cm) high, depending on the particular clone, with strong black spines on the edges. The flower spike, produced in May, is a long-lasting cylindrical head of bright yellow flowers cupped in brilliant red stem bracts. It is very free-flowering and produces offsets on strong prickly stolons.

A. orlandiana. This Brazilian species forms a stiff upright rosette of yellow-green leaves cross-banded with dark brown. It requires more warmth in winter than many aechmeas.

A. pineliana. This Central American species is a rosette about 2 ft (60 cm) across, with dark green leaves banded silver below and with black spines on their edges. The dense spike of yellow flowers is surrounded by bright red bracts, while the floral bracts have light brown bristles at their tips, giving a teazle-like appearance. The leaves will become red in a good light, particularly at flowering time, which is usually May or June.

A. 'Royal Wine'. A soft-leaved plant, this generally produces its flowers in summer, followed by long-lasting berries. Offsets are freely borne on stolons. It should have a winter temperature of 50°F (10°C).

24

Above: the popular urn plant, *Aechmea fasciata*, is ideal for beginners and may be grown on into a multi-headed specimen after flowering

Below: the vivid flower head of *A. chantinii* (left) persists for several weeks; *A.cylindrata* (right) is very free flowering in summer

A. weilbachii var. leodiensis. The soft green leaves are often tinted with maroon-red. It likes a minimum temperature of 55°F (13°C) and will flower in fairly shady conditions.

OTHER SPECIES AND RELATED PLANTS

Many other species of *Aechmea* are seen in collections and at shows, but, before being tempted to buy an unknown plant, you should find out its ultimate size; some may grow to 3 ft (90 cm) or more in diameter and could become an embarrassment in a small greenhouse or home. Other plants related to *Aechmea* are encountered from time to time, such as *Hohenbergia*, *Portea* and *Streptocalyx*. These too tend to be rather large for the average grower and mostly require a winter temperature of 60°F (15°C).

Above: the flower spike of *Aechmea nudicaulis* (left) remains showy for a long period; the hybrid *A.* 'Royal Wine' (right) has brightly coloured berries and a rosette of flexible glossy leaves

Below: *A. weilbachii* var. *leodiensis* (left), a soft-leaved plant which prefers some shade; the Brazilian *A. orlandiana* (right) should have a winter temperature of 60°F (15°C)

Billbergia

Billbergias are closely allied to *Aechmea* and need the same cultural treatment as the hard-leaved members of that genus, like *Aechmea fasciata*. Their distribution in nature is through Central America from southern Mexico to Argentina and they are usually found as epiphytes, growing into large clumps in open situations near the edge of forests, where they receive strong light. Most species form stiff, upright, cylindrical tubes, in contrast to the open rosettes of aechmeas, and need as much light as possible short of scorching. The leaves are tough, edged with strong spines, often banded with silver-grey and, in some cases, blotched and marbled with red and white as well. The flower spikes are striking, in shades of blue, green and yellow, shown off by large pink or red stem bracts. Unlike *Aechmea*, the flowers are comparatively short-lived, lasting only one or two weeks. Nearly all species have a definite flowering time, most of them blooming in the spring.

Almost without exception, billbergias will stand a temperature of 45°F (7°C) in the winter, if kept dry, and they are equally at home in pots or on a bromeliad tree, in the home, conservatory or greenhouse. During the summer months, most of them can be put outside in a lightly shaded position, where the colour of the leaves is enhanced, with many developing a strong red tinge.

About 1¼ ft (38 cm) tall, the hybrid *Billbergia* 'Fantasia' has green and red leaves marbled with cream

Billbergia pyramidalis var. *concolor* is very easy to grow and increase

After flowering, most *Billbergia* produce their offsets quite close to the parent plant. The easiest way to remove them is to tip the whole plant out of its pot and tease away the soil around the base. The pups can then be detached readily with a sideways and downwards pressure, while the old plant may be repotted to produce more offsets. The pups are potted into a sand and moss peat mixture in 3 in. (7.5 cm) pots. Water them only when the compost is dry and they should flower the following season.

B. amoena. This Brazilian species is a stiff tubular plant about 1½ ft (45 cm) tall and 2 in. (5 cm) in diameter. The green leaves, suffused with red and marbled with cream, have distinct silver bands across them and small brown spines at the edges.

Above and below: the Brazilian *Quesnelia liboniana* the commonest species of this genus and the first to be introduced, in the mid-nineteenth century

The upright spike carries a few yellow-green flowers margined with blue, set off by several large pink bracts, appearing in January or February. The offsets grow close to the parent plant on very short, thick stolons and may be left so that the plant eventually makes an attractive clump of almost pipe-like tubes.

B. chlorosticta. Known to gardeners for many years as *B. saundersii*, this has slightly arching, narrow 1½ ft (45 cm) leaves of brownish green, with copious cream-white spotting and banding when grown in a good light. It forms an upright rosette, from the centre of which the slightly drooping flower spike is produced in May, with bright red stem bracts and a large panicle of red and violet flowers. Offsets grow quite close to the parent as in *B. nutans* and, like them, should flower after one season of growth.

B. 'Muriel Waterman'. This is one of many beautiful hybrids developed by the great American collector and enthusiast, Mulford Foster. The stout tubular rosette, about 3 in. (7.5 cm) in diameter, opens out to a funnel at the top of some six to eight leaves. These are rose-maroon with transverse silver bands, making it one of the most colourful foliage billbergias. The showy flower spike consists of pink bracts and yellow flowers edged with steel-blue.

B. nutans. Probably the most commonly grown bromeliad, this will survive almost freezing temperatures if it is dry. It flowers regularly in spring, bearing a drooping spike of yellow-green flowers edged with blue. The stem carries several deep pink, papery bracts below the flower head. The tufted rosette is made up of about 15 grey-green, narrow, tapering leaves 1½ ft (45 cm) long. Offsets are produced on short stolons and root easily.

B. porteana. Within the genus is a distinct group of billbergias whose flowers have tightly coiled petals, of which this species is fairly typical. It is tall, up to 3 ft (90 cm), forming a tube 3 in. (7.5 cm) in diameter of six to eight leaves, recurving slightly at the tips, dull green, mealy-banded on the back and edged with spines. The flower stem, appearing in August, is about as tall as the leaves and carries several 6 in. (15 cm) bright red bracts, while the drooping panicle is up to 1 ft (30 cm) long, with green flowers margined in violet. These are followed by large ridged ovaries covered with silver-grey wool, which last several months and usually give fertile seed. Seeds may be sown (see p.20) to produce flowering plants in three years. Offsets generally take two years to flower.

B. pyramidalis. This Brazilian species differs from most others in the genus in that it flowers low down in the centre of the rosette. The flower head of pink and purple is enclosed in an open flattish rosette of grey-green leaves, each 2 in. (5 cm) wide and 10 in. (25 cm) long, with rather blunt tips. The offsets are produced on strong 4 to 6 in. (10–15 cm) stolons and, if not removed, a plant can soon cover quite a large area. The variety *concolor* has pale green, glossy leaves and a central flower head of "dayglo" pink.

QUESNELIA

The genus *Quesnelia* is very similar to *Billbergia*, forming somewhat stiff, upright rosettes and being just as easy to grow. However, most *Quesnelia* have spine-edged and spine-tipped leaves and are less attractive as houseplants for this reason. The species most often seen is *Quesnelia liboniana*. It is a narrow, few-leaved, upright tube, 1½ ft (45 cm) tall, with spine-edged grey-green leaves. The flower spike has a red stem and blue and red flowers in April, sometimes followed by orange-yellow berries. The pups form at the ends of long, very spiny stolons.

Cryptanthus

The *Cryptanthus* species and hybrids have earned the name of earth stars on account of their shape. They make very flat rosettes of 10 to 30 tapering pointed leaves that hug the ground, varying in size from the 3 in. (7.5 cm) diameter of *Cryptanthus roseus* to the 2 ft (60 cm) of *C. fosterianus* and its hybrids. They are excellent houseplants for warm rooms and the smaller species are widely used in bottle gardens, where they will outlive most other plants without increasing in size too much (see also the Wisley handbook, *Houseplants,* for information about bottle gardens). In the greenhouse earth stars need a winter minimum temperature of 60°F (15°C). In nature they are inhabitants of Brazil, growing in rich leafy material on the forest floor, and in cultivation they should therefore be given a similar, rich, open compost. A mixture of well-rotted leafmould, coarse sand and moss peat in equal volumes seems to suit them, enabling the roots to remain damp but not wet for most of the time. The amount of light required depends on the particular species and some need fairly heavy shade to bring out the best colours. Light is an important factor in determining their colours, so it is well worth experimenting to obtain the appearance that you prefer.

All earth stars produce small white flowers in the central leaf axils, mostly in summer. These are quite short-lived and soon wither away, while tiny new plants emerge. The pups grow very quickly and are easily detached to form new plants (see p.20).

C. acaulis. This small species is happier in fairly strong light, where it grows into a rosette about 3 in. (7.5 cm) across, consisting of a dozen or so leaves, red-brown, stiff and wavy-edged, with many tiny grey scales on their surface. It survives much drier conditions than many other earth stars.

C. bivittatus. Frequently grown, particularly in bottle gardens, this is one of the smaller species. It forms a rosette of 15 to 25 leaves, 2 to 3 in. (5–7.5 cm) long and tapering to a point, with the edges waved and spined. In shade, the leaves are yellow-green with central and marginal stripes of dark green; in stronger light, they are tinged with bright pink, particularly at the base; and in bright light, the whole plant becomes reddish pink and loses much of the green.

Opposite, above: like other species, *Cryptanthus bivittatus* changes colour according to the amount of light

Below: *C. bromelioides* var. *tricolor* is sometimes called the rainbow plant and should be grown in plenty of light to produce the best colours

Cryptanthus zonatus is a medium-sized plant with very decorative spine-edged leaves

C. beuckerii. Growing a rosette about 4 in. (10 cm) across, this rather upright plant has unusual paddle-shaped leaves marbled in green and brown. It is happiest in shade. Offsets are freely produced in the leaf axils on short stolons.

C. bromelioides. This is more upright in growth than most members of the genus, and has stiff, tapering, recurving, brown leaves produced at short intervals up a rigid stem, with a total spread of about 1 ft (30 cm). The species itself is not very often seen, but the variety *tricolor* is a popular houseplant. In this, the leaves are beautifully variegated with longitudinal stripes of green, brown and cream and shaded bright pink over much of the surface. It needs strong light to bring out the best colours. A peculiarity seems to be its extreme shyness of flowering, although offsets are freely produced from the leaf axils throughout the year.

C. 'Cascade'. This American hybrid with bright red-brown leaves requires strong light. It is best grown in a hanging basket, since the 8 in (20 cm) diameter rosette produces offsets on long stolons, which are not easily detached.

C. fosterianus. This is one of the largest species, sometimes attaining 2 ft (60 cm) across. To reach this size, it really needs a minimum temperature of 70°F (21°C) and a very rich compost. However, it will easily grow to 1 ft (30 cm) in diameter with 60°F (15°C). The dozen or so long tapering leaves that comprise the rosette are mainly red-brown, adorned with numerous zig-zag silver bands across the face,

34

and are very stiff, almost artificial-looking. Like all *Cryptanthus*, it is a good plant for a bromeliad tree. There are many hybrids of this zebra-like species.

C. roseus.   This small earth star delights in a shady position. It makes a rosette of 20 to 30 very narrow, pointed, wavy-edged leaves in a delicate cafe-au-lait colour, shaded pink at their bases. The rosette is 3 in. (7.5 cm) across, long-lasting and, with its many leaves, producing a large number of offsets which are easily grown on.

C. zonatus.   This Brazilian species has broad, very stiff, wavy leaves with striking zebra-like banding. There are a number of varieties with different-coloured leaves, including *viridis*, green with silver bands, and *fuscus*, red-brown with silver bands. All need good light and a minimum winter temperature of 55°F (13°C).

× CRYPTBERGIA

Cryptanthus have been crossed with *Billbergia* and the resulting hybrids are intermediate in habit between the two genera. One of the commonest in cultivation, probably because it is so easy to grow, is × *Cryptbergia rubra*. It forms a stiff rosette about 9 in. (23 cm) across of 20 to 30 hard, recurving, tapering leaves, glossy mahogany-red on top, silvery grey beneath. The dense stemless flower head in the centre of the plant has the yellow and blue flowers of *Billbergia nutans* and lasts a week in colour. Offsets are produced on short stolons and root easily, to flower in one year. It likes a peat and sand compost, with regular feeding at every third watering, and very bright light – almost full sun. A temperature of 45°F (7°C) does not trouble this plant at all.

Neoregelia

This is a genus of light-loving plants, mainly inhabitants of Brazil and epiphytic in nature, which have fairly stiff leaves, often with red marbling. There are numerous sports of some species, in particular of N. meyendorffii, with longitudinal bands of white or cream along the leaves. They are tank-forming, that is to say, the rosettes hold water in the cup formed by the leaves at the centre of the plant. The flowers are generally pink to purple, massed in a head nestling in the centre of the rosette – hence the common name of bird's nest for this group of bromeliads. The many florets in a single flower head open two or three at a time over a period of several weeks, each one lasting only a day or two. Neoregelias are remarkable in that, just before flowering and often for several months, the whole central area of the plant becomes coloured, usually in a shade of red, being brightest at the base of the leaves and suffusing much of the leaf surface.

After flowering, offsets are mostly produced on stolons from the leaf axils, allowing plenty of room for new rosettes to develop. This is especially noticeable with the dwarf, more tubular, rosette-forming species, where a new plant may arise on a long thin stolon some distance from the parent, giving a very spidery appearance to a mature clump.

Neoregelias are easy plants to grow in the house or greenhouse, in pots or on a bromeliad tree. They should be placed in good light, but avoiding direct sunlight. Water them only when the compost is dry, feed with a high potash fertilizer at every third watering and, if the central cup is allowed to retain water in the summer, make sure that this is flushed out every couple of weeks to prevent stagnation. A suitable potting compost is composed of equal volumes of coarse sand and moss peat. Winter temperatures of 45°F (7°C) will satisfy them if they are kept dry during the coldest periods. Offsets usually take two years to flower.

N. concentrica. A Brazilian species, this attains 1½ ft (45 cm) across and has broad, dark green leaves and mauve colouring in the central area at flowering time. It requires the same treatment as N. meyendorffii.

Opposite, above: Neoregelia meyendorffii var. variegata is a striking and robust houseplant

Below: the fingernail plant, N. spectabilis, bears small blue flowers in the centre of the rosette

N. fosteriana.   This forms a thin, tubular, upright rosette of yellow-green leaves banded with light brown and slightly reflexed at the top. The bird's nest of mauve flowers is produced deep in the tube of leaves and offsets grow at the ends of long wiry stolons.

N. marmorata.   This species has a rosette composed of up to 30 fairly stiff leaves, 1 ft (30 cm) long, which are green marbled with red-brown and turn brilliant red when the flower head is produced. It should be given as much light as possible for the most vivid colour. The offsets appear on stolons about 2 in. (5 cm) long and take two years to flower.

N. meyendorffii (*N. carolinae*).   Grown from seed to flower in two to three years and produced in thousands for the houseplant market, this tough, almost people-proof plant is widely used for interior decoration in homes, foyers and shopping arcades. In flower, it is an open rosette of green leaves, 1¼ to 1½ ft (38–45 cm) in diameter, with the whole central area a brilliant wax-like red, enclosing the bird's nest flower head of mauve florets. The variegated leaf forms are spectacular and are quite readily available, even though they must be propagated by offsets.

N. spectabilis.   The fingernail plant, as it is called, has purplish brown leaves with silver-grey lines across the backs and bright pink tips. They form a semi-open rosette about 1 ft (30 cm) across, but do not change colour at flowering time. The bird's nest flowers are blue. One of the hardiest species, it is best grown in strong light.

N. tigrina.   This species grows new plants at the end of long stolons and resembles *N. tristis* (below) in shape, but is even smaller. It has tiny tubular rosettes ¾ in. (2 cm) in diameter with slightly flaring tips. The leaves are shining green, banded heavily with mahogany.

N. tristis.   Although of similar colouring to *N. marmorata* (above), this has a quite different rosette. About 10 leaves make a narrow tubular base, which rises to a height of 5 in. (12.5 cm) and then opens out at the top to 6 in. (15 cm) across. The bird's nest head of blue flowers is sunk deep in the tube. New rosettes are produced on long thin stolons and often develop roots in mid-air. It is a particularly good plant for a bromeliad tree, climbing by means of the long stolons.

Nidularium

This small genus from Brazil is often confused with *Neoregelia*, owing to the similarity of the bird's nest type of flower head. In *Nidularium*, however, this is surrounded by coloured bracts and the whole assembly is a distinct separate entity on its own stem, rather than being buried in the rosette. A further difference is that the true leaves of the rosette do not colour as they do in *Neoregelia*.

Nidularium form open rosettes of broad flexible leaves, most in the range of 1 to 2 ft (30–60 cm) in diameter, and have bird's nest flower heads of white or purple flowers with a collar of brilliantly coloured bract leaves. The rather soft texture of the leaves indicates that the plants need a significant amount of shade and they do not like temperatures below 50°F (10°C). The potting compost can be the usual sand and moss peat mixture suitable for most bromeliads. Regular feeding is required throughout the period of growth and should also continue after flowering, to provide food for the production of offsets, which mostly develop close in the leaf axils. Like other bromeliads, each species of *Nidularium* has its own flowering time. Pups take one or two years to reach flowering size.

Since these bromeliads grow and flower in quite shady positions, they make excellent houseplants. In the home, water them only when the compost is dry and site them well away from a source of heat, such as a fire or radiator. They will then be very rewarding plants, maintaining a good shape and not becoming drawn as so many other plants do in shade. In the greenhouse, make sure that they are well shaded and certainly do not give them direct sunlight. A north-facing conservatory is ideal, perhaps in the company of foliage begonias, ferns and shade-loving plants.

N. billbergioides.   This is an upright rosette, about 1 ft (30 cm) high, of glossy, light green leaves 1 in. (2.5 cm) wide. The flower spike rises above the leaves and consists of white flowers 2 in. (5 cm) across, enclosed in bright yellow bracts which last for about six weeks. After flowering, the offsets grow on stolons 3 to 4 in. (7.5–10 cm) long. There are varieties with bracts of different colours, from pale yellow to very dark red. This plant is frequently offered in shops and is an excellent houseplant.

N. burchellii.   This nidularium is distinct from all other species. The rather upright rosette is made up of 10 to 12 leaves, which are dull green above, purple below, reflexing at the ends and 10 in. (25 cm) long. Held just above the leaves, the flower head comprises white flowers and small green bracts, the whole being

Above: *Nidularium billbergioides* is unusual in having the flower head on a long stalk

Below: *N. regelioides* is a 2 ft (60 cm) rosette of leathery leaves with red flowers and needs a fairly shady position

almost globular in shape and usually appearing in the late autumn. As the flowers fade, they are replaced by green berries, which soon turn bright orange and remain colourful for several months and well into the new year. It is a very showy little plant. New plants develop at the end of wiry stolons 3 to 6 in. (7.5–15 cm) long and root to flower the next year.

N. chloromarchellii. Of similar size to *N. innocentii* (below), this has leaves shiny green above and rust-red beneath. The blue and white flowers are backed up by orange-red bracts. It seems to set seed easily, the small brown seeds being encased in jelly within long fleshy berries which develop in the central flower head.

N. fulgens. This is a rosette about 1 ft (30 cm) in diameter, rather more upright than most species, of pale green, glossy leaves slightly marbled with darker green. The brilliant flower head lasts some weeks.

N. innocentii. This is an open rosette of 30 or so leaves, green on the upper surface, dark purple underneath, reaching a diameter of 1½ ft (45 cm) and forming a water-retaining cup in the centre. At flowering time a bird's nest head of white flowers develops, which is surrounded by stiff red-purple bracts. There are several varieties of this species, with the leaves plain green or variously striped along their length with white or cream.

The pillar-box red head of bract-leaves of *Nidularium fulgens*

Tillandsia

Tillandsia is a very large genus of bromeliads, distributed in nature from southern North America, through Central and South America, to Argentina, in both moist forests and dry desert-like areas. Most are epiphytic, except for a few giant saxicolous (growing on rocks) species. For cultural treatment, they may be divided into three main groups, which are easily distinguished by their appearance.

GREY-LEAVED PLANTS

Commonly known as air plants, most tilliandsias available in Britain are of the xerophytic type – that is, existing with little water. They are mainly small and have grey leaves, owing to a covering of tiny peltate scales which constitute the water-absorbing mechanism of the plants. Watering, therefore, amounts to daily spraying or dipping the plants in water, preferably rainwater, to wet the leaves thoroughly. The addition of a high potash fertilizer to the water at every third watering during the summer months is advisable. A winter minimum temperature of 50°F (10°C) is adequate for the majority of this group, with some of them able to withstand temperatures down to freezing point if kept dry. They need a light position in the greenhouse or home at all times of the year.

Being epiphytic and xerophytic, these tillandsias are difficult to grow in pots, which prevent their roots and bases from drying out quickly enough, although they can be treated in the same way as orchids, using bark or osmunda fibre as the potting medium. It is much easier to grow them on a piece of bark or branch, where, if they are first tied or even glued on, they will soon develop a few strong wiry roots with which to attach themselves firmly. Most of the plants offered for sale are imported from the wild, since they are slow to increase from offsets and take several years to reach flowering size from seed. However, they establish readily if mounted on bark or a bromeliad tree. Provided they are not overwatered and are grown in a light airy position, they make an attractive showpiece indoors.

Opposite: *Tillandsia lindenii*, a spectacular plant but sometimes reluctant to flower

Tillandsia brachycaulos, one of the epiphytic species which should be grown on bark with good air circulation

T. argentea (*T. tectorum*).   A tufted plant, from Central America and the West Indies, this has numerous, narrow, silver-grey leaves 3 in. (7.5 cm) long. The flower spike is 6 in. (15 cm) tall, with about six pale violet florets.

T. brachycaulos.   This species has a dense rosette of some 30 leaves, 6 to 9 in. (15–23 cm) long, heavily scaled and silver tinged with red-brown. A dense head of lilac flowers is borne in the centre in spring. It is found over a wide area of Mexico and Central America.

T. bulbosa.   This is an example of a tillandsia with a bulb-like base. It has a tubular rosette and the silver-grey leaves flare out at the top. It is very variable, ranging in height from 2 in. to 1 ft (5–30 cm). The flower spike consists of two to eight blue or violet flowers held just above the leaves in summer.

T. caulescens.   This Peruvian species develops a long, branching, woody stem, up to 1½ ft (45 cm) long. At the end is a tuft of 4 in. (10 cm) grey leaves, from the centre of which appears a spike of about a dozen white flowers with red bracts.

T. crocata.   This has almost round silver-grey leaves about 6 in. (15 cm) long and produces a spike of a few yellow flowers with green bracts in the late summer. It needs particular care in watering and strong light.

T. gardnerii.   This is 10 in. (25 cm) in diameter, with curving, narrow, grey-scaled leaves, and produces a compound spike of 4 to 12 heads of rose and lavender flowers in summer.

T. ionantha.   This is one of the smallest species and is readily available. A compact plant about 2 in. (5 cm) high and the same across, it has 30 to 40 very stiff, silver-grey, pointed leaves and will make a tight clump in a few years. At flowering time, in late spring, the whole plant becomes brilliant red, while purple and red flowers with prominent anthers protrude from the centre of the rosette. The colour lasts for several weeks. It is a robust plant and will succeed with a winter temperature of 40°F (5°C).

T. plumosa.   This is very silvery and feathery in appearance and has a dense head of violet flowers in late summer. A beautiful Mexican species, it makes a rosette only 2 in. (5 cm) in diameter.

Tillandsia caulescens is a good species for beginners

Tillandsia crocata has its silver-grey leaves so tightly curled in as to be almost cylindrical

45

T. stricta. Slightly larger, this forms a ball about 3 in. (7.5 cm) in diameter, composed of 50 to 60 narrow, recurving, grey leaves. In May it bears a 3 in. (7.5 cm) spike of pink and purple flowers, persisting for two weeks or so. This is usually followed by two or three offsets from among the basal leaves, which themselves will flower the following year. It is easily grown and will withstand a temperature of 40°F (5°C).

T. usneoides. One of the most amazing plants of all is the Spanish moss, which forms long festoons of grey-green matted stems and leaves. The individual strands are almost hair-like but, if examined closely, they prove to have typical *Tillandsia* leaves covered with small moisture-retaining scales and produce miniature, three-petalled, greenish white flowers. The bundles of stems are easily divided to make new festoons. In cultivation, it will stand low temperatures, down to 40°F (5°C), but it is essential to provide plenty of fresh air. Water both morning and evening, with rainwater if possible, and grow it in a light position, draped over a branch or similar support.

PARTLY SCALE-LEAVED PLANTS

There are a few species of *Tillandsia* with thin, somewhat scaled leaves that are often available as houseplants in pots. They can be grown to flowering size in 4 in. (10 cm) pots of a peat and sand mixture and should be watered when dry, fertilized regularly and kept in a light but not sunny position in the house or greenhouse. They require a winter minimum temperature of 50°F (10°C). Offsets are produced fairly close in the leaf axils before and after flowering and are quite easily detached to root in peat and sand during the summer.

T. anceps. This is a 1 ft (30 cm) rosette of green leaves striped with fine brown lines at the base. The pink and green head of bracts is very similar to *T. lindenii* (below), but the blue flowers are only 1 in. (2.5 cm) across. White-flowered plants are sometimes seen. It will accept a little more shade than most species.

T. flabellata. This makes a rosette about 1 ft (30 cm) across, the narrow leaves green with silvery undersides and the flower head consisting of 8 to 12 separate spikes from a central stem, held above the leaves. Each spike is a brilliant orange, spear-shaped bract head and violet flowers with yellow anthers appear from the edges. The spike remains in colour for four to six weeks.

T. lindenii (*T. cyanea*). This popular plant is a 1 ft (30 cm) rosette of red-brown leaves, silver-scaled beneath. The central flower spike is a flat spearhead shape, a wax-like bract of pink and green from the edges of which bright blue 2 in. (5 cm) flowers emerge one after another, each lasting only two or three days, but the whole blooming for about a month in early summer.

Opposite, above: the miniature *Tillandsia ionantha* (left) and slightly larger *T. stricta* (right) will both accept low temperatures
Below: *T. bergerii* (left) and *T. streptophylla* (right) have grey- and brown-scaled leaves respectively

All are xerophytic and should be sprayed with rainwater daily, being excellent for a bromeliad tree in a well-lit position

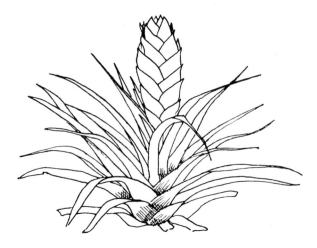

Tillandsia anceps has a spear-shaped flower head of green and pink resembling *T. lindenii*, with smaller blue flowers

Below: the strong-growing *Tillandsia tenuifolia* is able to withstand low temperatures and a wide variety of conditions and is an easy plant to grow

Tillandsia multicaulis is a soft-leaved species, one of the few to produce several flower spikes at once

SOFT-LEAVED PLANTS

Finally, there are the soft-leaved *Tillandsia* originating from moist tropical forests. Some species and hybrids of this group are being introduced here as houseplants by European growers. In cultivation, they need shade and a temperature of 60°F (15°C) and should be watered and fed in the same way as other shade-loving bromeliads like *Nidularium* and *Vriesea*. They generally produce a good number of offsets from the leaf axils after flowering, which may be rooted individually in 3 in. (7.5 cm) pots of peat and sand during the summer, when the temperature is not likely to fall below 68°F (20°C), or at any time of year in a heated propagator.

T. leiboldiana. This makes a rosette 1 to 1½ ft (30–45 cm) across of 20 to 30 soft green leaves, sometimes dark at the base and speckled with maroon. The upright branched spike of vermilion-red bracts holding lilac flowers is long-lasting and wax-like in appearance.

Other soft-leaved kinds, such as *Tillandsia multicaulis*, have simple or compound flower heads, usually adorned with showy red bracts and yellow or violet flowers.

49

Vriesea and Guzmania

Vriesea and *Guzmania* are mostly inhabitants of rain forests in Central and South America. They are similar in appearance, forming fairly open rosettes of soft leaves, and in their requirements, needing light shade and a winter minimum temperature of 60°F (15°C). They are grown from seed in large numbers in Europe for sale as houseplants, for which purpose they are superb, with long-lasting flower heads and often with coloured foliage. Although plants from 1 to 3 ft (30–90 cm) across or more are available, it is the smaller kinds that are generally offered. Most are grown in pots, using a rich free-draining compost: a mixture of equal volumes of leafmould, coarse grit or perlite and moss peat is suitable. Water when the compost is dry and feed with a liquid fertilizer at every third watering. Many of them have a water-retaining cup in the centre and, as mentioned earlier, this is best kept empty of water if they are grown as houseplants or if the temperature is likely to fall below 50°F (10°C).

V. carinata. A small Brazilian species some 8 in. (20 cm) across, this has a rosette made up of about 20 pale green, shiny leaves. The long-lasting flower spike is wax-like, with yellow flowers appearing from the edges of the red and yellow fan-shaped bract head in February or March. It will survive 50°F (10°C) in winter if the central cup is kept dry. After flowering, offsets are freely produced, which root easily and may be flowered in one year.

V. hieroglyphica. Often seen on sale, this is a beautiful plant with broad, glossy green leaves crossbanded with many irregular, fine brown lines. It grows quickly under warm conditions, but takes several years to reach flowering size. By this time, it is a rosette some 3 ft (90 cm) across, with 50 or 60 leaves, and needs a fair amount of space. The flower spike is 3 ft (90 cm) high, carrying tubular green bracts with yellow flowers.

V. rodigasiana. When not in flower, this plant is similar in size and shape to *V. carinata* (above). However, the spike is an upright stem 1 ft (30 cm) high, with single, cylindrical, bright yellow, waxen bracts at intervals up it, from which are produced large yellow flowers. The spike remains colourful for several weeks. Many pups appear after flowering and take two years to flower.

V. splendens. The flaming sword is commonly seen, either as a plant in flower or as a small seedling for use in bottle gardens. A small 4 in. (10 cm) plant is normally about a year old from seed and will need a further two years of growth to reach flowering size. A plant in flower is a rosette some 1 ft (30 cm) in diameter, with a central flower stem carrying a flat spear-like bract head of shining orange-red, from the edges of which yellow flowers emerge one at a time over a period of four to

Opposite: *Vriesea carinata*, an undemanding plant which is suitable for a bromeliad tree

51

Above: *Vriesea hieroglyphica* is an excellent foliage houseplant

Below: two hybrid vrieseas, 'Mariae' (left) with bright green leaves and 'Polonia' (right) with a branched flower spike

Opposite: *Guzmania lingulata* var. *cardinalis* has red bracts

six weeks. The leaves are very ornamental, 2 in. (5 cm) wide and green with broad, irregular, brown bands. Recently developed hybrids have more brilliantly coloured leaves and some have flower spikes with branched stems, each carrying a coloured spearhead. These hybrids, like the species itself, usually produce only one offset after flowering and plants obtained are generally grown from seed.

V. tesselata (*V. gigantea*). This has ornamental foliage of blue-green with fine yellow-brown markings, but grows fairly large, some 3 ft (90 cm) high and wide, and takes several years to reach flowering size.

G. lingulata. One of the commonest guzmanias, this forms a 10 in. (25 cm) rosette of pale green, glossy, slightly reflexing leaves, from the centre of which rises a stout stem carrying a head of white flowers surrounded by brilliant yellow bracts. There are also varieties with orange or red bracts, the red-bracted ones often having red toning in the leaves. Commercially, they are grown from seed to flower in two years. Offsets are freely produced after flowering, which root quickly to flower the next season. A winter temperature of 50°F (10°C) will suit them, with light shading. They are very accommodating houseplants.

G. monostachya. This is a rosette of bright, pale green, 1 ft (30 cm) long leaves. The strong upright flower head is cylindrical, pointed at the top, with red, black and green bracts and white flowers. It requires a temperature of 60°F (15°C) in winter, with a little shade, and is summer-flowering.

G. musaica. As a foliage plant, this is very effective indoors, with its broad green leaves crossbanded with brown to form a rosette about 2 ft (60 cm) across. The flower spike is a compact, somewhat rounded head of orange-yellow inflated bracts with large, pale yellow flowers. It likes fairly heavy shade and a winter temperature of 60°F (15°C). Offsets are rather sparingly produced after flowering, so most plants are raised from seed, the seedlings taking three years to reach flowering size.

G. zahnii. This is a larger plant, growing to 3 ft (90 cm) across, with broad, yellowish-green leaves, striped with fine maroon lines on the undersides and red at their bases. The upright flower spike consists of red and yellow flowers and very large, reflexing, red bracts. It comes from Costa Rica and needs a temperature of 60°F (15°C) in winter. It is a striking plant in flower and has been the parent of many showy hybrids used as houseplants. It may be propagated by offsets during the summer months.

Opposite: *Guzmania zahnii* has a brilliant flower spike which stays colourful for weeks

Above: *Guzmania* 'Memoria', like a bigger version of *G. lingulata* with red bracts

Below: *G. sanguinea* may have red, orange or yellow bracts

Terrestrial bromeliads

As opposed to the majority of epiphytic bromeliads, some are found as true terrestrials growing in the ground, generally in open country where they receive maximum light. Many are fairly large and armed with fierce spines and are not really suitable as houseplants. A cool greenhouse is the best abode for most of them, where they would associate well with desert cacti.

ANANAS

The best known and most important of the terrestrials is the pineapple, *Ananas comosus*, which has become naturalized in many tropical regions of the world. There are numerous subspecies and varieties with various sizes and shapes of fruit and different foliage, including attractive variegated leaf forms. All need similar treatment, with as much light and heat as possible.

To root a pineapple top from a bought fruit, choose the warmest time in summer. Remove the small rosette from the top of the fruit and cut away any residual pineapple flesh. Take off some of the lower leaves to leave a short woody stem base and allow this to dry off for two or three days. Then pot it into a mixture of equal volumes of moss peat and coarse sand to come just up to the bottom of the remaining leaves, in a 4 in. (10 cm) pot. Water it in, do not cover with a polythene bag and keep it in as warm a place as possible, where it will get maximum light – on a shelf by a window, for instance, or near the glass in a greenhouse. Water only when the compost has become dry, bearing in mind that this will happen quickly in the warm light conditions. In summer, roots should begin to form in four to six weeks and, when this occurs, a high potash fertilizer like Tomorite may be added to the water at every third watering. Once the plant starts to produce new leaves from the top, it will have quite a strong root system and will need potting on into a 6 in. (15 cm) pot, using a rich compost of equal volumes of moss peat, sand and well-rotted garden compost. It must then be grown in the warmest place possible, certainly not less than 60°F (15°C) in winter, with the maximum amount of light, even direct sunlight.

On average, a pineapple grows to 3 ft (90 cm) or so in diameter, with very tough, spine-edged leaves, and may well produce fruit after two or three years. It then has a manner of growth like other

One of the many forms of the pineapple, *Ananas comosus*

bromeliads and will give offsets from the leaf axils, which are rooted more easily than fruit tops. Offsets are sometimes produced from around the tuft of leaves on the top of the fruit and these may also be used for increase.

BROMELIA

Similar in growth to the pineapple and making large plants with very spiny, stout, recurved leaves are members of the genus *Bromelia*, which is mainly native to Brazil. The flower spike is usually red and purple and forms a brilliant head of colour low in the centre of the rosette, followed by yellow or orange berries. They are very striking in flower, but tend to become too large for the average greenhouse or home. Treatment is the same as for the pineapple.

FASCICULARIA

Another genus with extremely spiny leaves and growing rather too big for pot culture is *Fascicularia*, from Chile. However, in the southwest of England and other mild districts, *Fascicularia bicolor* appears to be hardy and may develop into a clump several feet across, of rosettes formed from narrow, spine-edged, grey-green leaves. It blooms in summer with a dense central head of blue and red set low in the middle of each rosette, while many of the central leaves turn a brilliant sealing-wax red.

PUYA

The puyas, some of which attain a height of 30 ft (9 m) in the South American Andes, include a few which are just about manageable in pots. One of these, *Puya alpestris*, is usually grown from seed, which germinates readily (see p.20). The seedlings grow quickly. needing a temperature of only 40°F (5°C) after they are three or four months old, but requiring good light at all times and not too much water. As they grow, they make very dense rosettes of narrow, grey-green, recurving leaves, edged with numerous strong spines. At two years from seed, they ought to be in 5 in. (12.5 cm) pots and will have a leaf spread of about 2 ft (60 cm). If potted on into larger pots, they will get even bigger.

Kept in the same pot, the plants will eventually flower, which is worth waiting for, although it may take five or six years from seed. The tall flower stem bears a compound spike of large green and light blue flowers and pink bracts, the whole flower head lasting about a month. It is a xerophytic bromeliad, inhabiting areas where water is scarce and maximum light is received. In cultivation, therefore, water only when the compost is dry and feed with a high potash fertilizer about once a month.

ABROMEITIELLA

At the other end of the size scale is *Abromeitiella brevifolia*, a xerophytic bromeliad from Argentina and Bolivia. It forms a large mound of tiny rosettes, each 2 in. (5 cm) in diameter, with stiff, grey-green, spiny 1 in. (2.5 cm) leaves and greenish white flower heads set among them. Its growth is very much like that of the cushion-forming saxifrages. Frost-free conditions are necessary for this little bromeliad, with as much light as possible and very little water.

DYCKIA and HECHTIA

These two genera require similar culture. The succulent-looking *Dyckia sulphurea (D. brevifolia)* has a rosette of 20 to 30 leaves, 4 to 5 in. (10–12.5 cm) long and tapering to a point, very thick and rigid with tiny toothed spines on the edges, pale green on top and silver with green lines beneath. The 1 to 1¼ ft (30–38 cm) stem bears eight to ten flowers spaced on the upper half, sulphur-yellow and wax-like. It is easily grown from seed to flower in about two years.

Hechtia argentea makes a dense mass of numerous rigid, silvery, spine-edged leaves upto 1½ ft (45 cm) long, finely scaled on the undersides. The flower spike is an open panicle of many small white flowers and light brown bracts. Like other xerophytic plants, it is easily grown in a peat and sand mixture with little water.

PITCAIRNIA

This large genus of bromeliads is not often seen outside specialist collections, even though some of the smaller ones can be grown easily in pots. Distributed in nature through Central and South America, they are nearly all terrestrial, with a few saxicolous and one or two epiphytic species. In appearance and cultivation needs, they may be divided into two groups.

In the first group are plants with soft, green, drooping, almost

Opposite: Pitcairnia ferruginea, the largest member of the genus, has long spine-edged leaves

grass-like leaves, spineless and forming large tufted clumps with a strong root system. Since all like acid soil, a peat and sand mixture with the addition of some leafmould is a satisfactory compost. They may be grown in pots or planted in a greenhouse bed or border, with a winter minimum temperature of 50°F (10°C), in a light but not sunny location. Watering is required only when the compost becomes dry. Much growth is made during the summer months, when they should be fed with a high potash fertilizer at every other watering. During the inactive winter period, water only at monthly intervals. Spikes of red, yellow, orange or white flowers are produced in summer, lasting about two weeks.

One of the smaller species is *Pitcairnia andreana*, which has tufts of narrow leaves 9 in. (23 cm) high, light green above and grey below. The upright flower spike carries 10 to 12 large orange-yellow flowers in June. Many offsets are produced, whether the plant is in flower or not, and a dense clump soon results. This is easily divided, as the divisions already have roots. In addition, the plant is self-fertile and sets seed freely.

Similar in its grass-like habit, *Pitcairnia maidifolia* is up to 3 ft (90 cm) tall and has an erect flower spike of white flowers surrounded by red and green bracts in July. There are many other species of the same shape but with different flower heads.

The second group is typified by *Pitcairnia pungens*. This is rarely more than 1¼ ft (38 cm) high and forms a somewhat bulbous, very spiny base. The deciduous green leaves are armed with strong brown spines and vary in length from 1 to 12 in. (2.5–30 cm). In autumn, the leaves fall off, leaving a spined bulbous base which must have a completely dry rest period from November to April, with a winter minimum temperature of 50°F (10°C). Watering should commence only when new leaf growth has started. Soon after this happens, a spike of orange-red flowers appears from the top of the bulb and offsets are produced simultaneously. *Pitcairnia nigra* is like *P. pungens*, but has vermilion-red flowers. This and other similar species are normally found growing on rocks in nature and therefore need a very open, free-draining compost, consisting of two parts of coarse sand and one part of moss peat by volume. They need stong light at all times.

A few pitcairnias, mostly the very large species like *Pitcairnia ferruginea*, resemble puyas with their heavily spined leaves and are difficult to distinguish until the flowers are produced.

Further information

RECOMMENDED READING

Bromeliads, W. Rauh. Blandford Press, London, 1979.
Bromeliads, Victoria Padilla. Crown Publishers, New York, 1986.

SUPPLIERS

Hollygate Nurseries, Ashington, West Sussex RH20 3BA.
Vesutor Ltd, Marringdean Rd, Billinghurst, West Sussex RH14 9EH.
B. Wall, 4 Selbourne Close, New Haw, Weybridge, Surrey KT15 3RG.
A. Schenkel, 2. Hamburg 55 – Blankenese, West Germany (seed).

SOCIETIES

Bromeliad Society of America, PO Box 3279, Santa Monica, California 90403, USA.

GLOSSARY

axil: angle formed by junction of leaf and stem
bract: modified leaf between the flower and the leaves
epiphytic: tree-dwelling, but not parasitic
peltate: shield-like, not attached at the edges
saxicolous: growing on rocks
stolon: strong sucker-like stem
terrestrial: growing on the ground
xerophytic: existing with little water